HORSE
POWER

SPARKY'S STEM GUIDE TO

TRAINS

BY KIRSTY HOLMES

KidHaven
PUBLISHING

Published in 2023 by **KidHaven Publishing, an Imprint of Greenhaven Publishing, LLC**
29 East 21st Street
New York, NY 10010

Edited by: Emilie Dufresne
Designed by: Danielle Jones

Cataloging-in-Publication Data

Names: Holmes, Kirsty.
Title: Sparky's STEM guide to trains / Kirsty Holmes.
Description: New York : KidHaven Publishing, 2023. |
Series: Horse power | Includes glossary and index.
Identifiers: ISBN 9781534540415 (pbk.) | ISBN 9781534540439 (library bound) | ISBN 9781534540422 (6 pack) | ISBN 9781534540446 (ebook)
Subjects: LCSH: Railroad trains--Juvenile literature.
Classification: LCC TF148.H635 2023 | DDC 625.2--dc23

Printed in the United States of America

CPSIA compliance information: Batch #CSKH23: For further information contact Greenhaven Publishing LLC, New York, New York at 1-844-317-7404.

Please visit our website, www.greenhavenpublishing.com. For a free color catalog of all our high-quality books, call toll free 1-844-317-7404 or fax 1-844-317-7405.

IMAGE CREDITS

All images are courtesy of Shutterstock.com, unless otherwise specified. With thanks to Getty Images, Thinkstock Photo and iStockphoto. Cover – NotionPic, A–R–T, logika600, BiterBig, Malchev, Alongkorn Sanguansook. 1 – BiterBig. 2 – Suiraton, Nadya_Art, NotionPic, Alongkorn Sanguansook. 3 – BiterBig. 4 – MuchMania. 5 – Mascha Tace. 6&7 – VectorShop, Volodimir Zozulinskyi, studioworkstock, VectorPot. 8&9 – Looper, Elvetica, Nucleartist. 10&11 – Flat vectors, VikiVector. 12 – mirrra3. 13 – Danielle Jones. 14 – AndriyAa. 15 – Laralova. 16 – WhiteDragon. 17 – Paul and Kate. 18 – supirloko89, Shanvood, VectorShow, Yuravector. 19 – vasilchuck, kostins, Azaze11o. 21 – ArtMalivanov, DRogatnev. 22 – Leremy, Juli92, Sergey Furtaev. 23 – Inspiring.

CONTENTS

WORDS THAT LOOK LIKE this CAN BE FOUND IN THE GLOSSARY ON PAGE 24.

WELCOME TO DRIVING SCHOOL!

ALL ABOARD! Hi there – I'm Jeremy Sparkplug, but you can call me Sparky. You must be the new crew. Welcome to the Horses for Courses School of Motoring!

Today, it's time to get your notebooks out, fellow trainspotters. We're going to be learning all about some really useful **vehicles** indeed: trains. Choo choo!

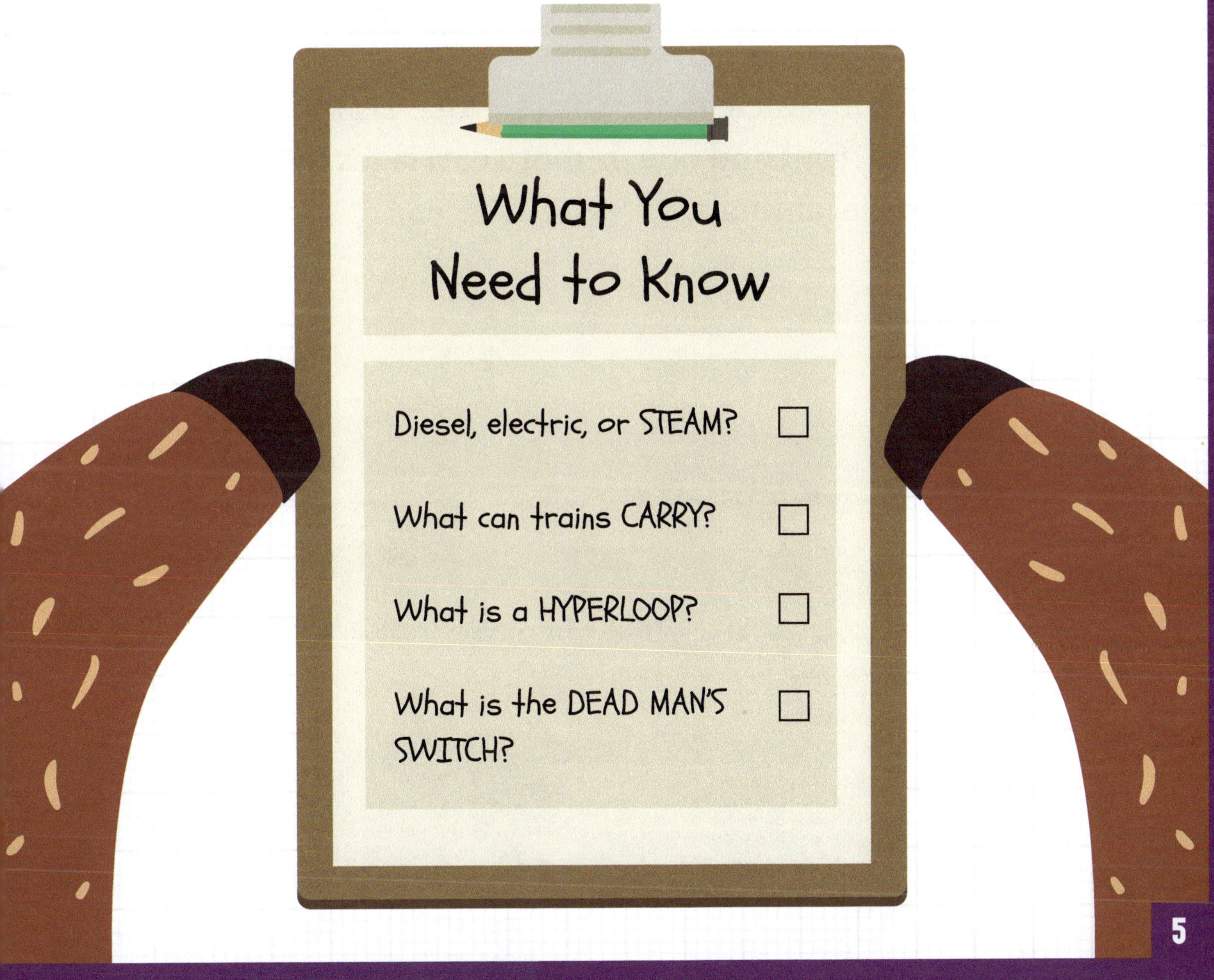

LESSON 1: WHAT IS A TRAIN?

A train is a type of vehicle that runs on **rails**. Trains have an **engine** at the front and one or more carriages behind for moving people, animals, or **freight**.

HORSES FOR COURSES
SCHOOL
EARN YOUR HORSESHOES
STEAM TRAIN
Meet Peggy – our friendly
train-driving unicorn!

LESSON 2:

TYPES OF TRAINS

STEAM TRAINS

Steam engines burn a **fuel**, such as coal, oil ,or wood, to heat water. The water turns to steam just like in a kettle, and the steam powers the engine.

DIESEL TRAINS

Diesel trains are powered by an engine. They run on liquid diesel fuel, similar to some cars. They only need one driver to operate.

THE FRONT OF THE TRAIN, WHICH CARRIES THE ENGINE AND PULLS THE CARRIAGES, IS CALLED A LOCOMOTIVE.

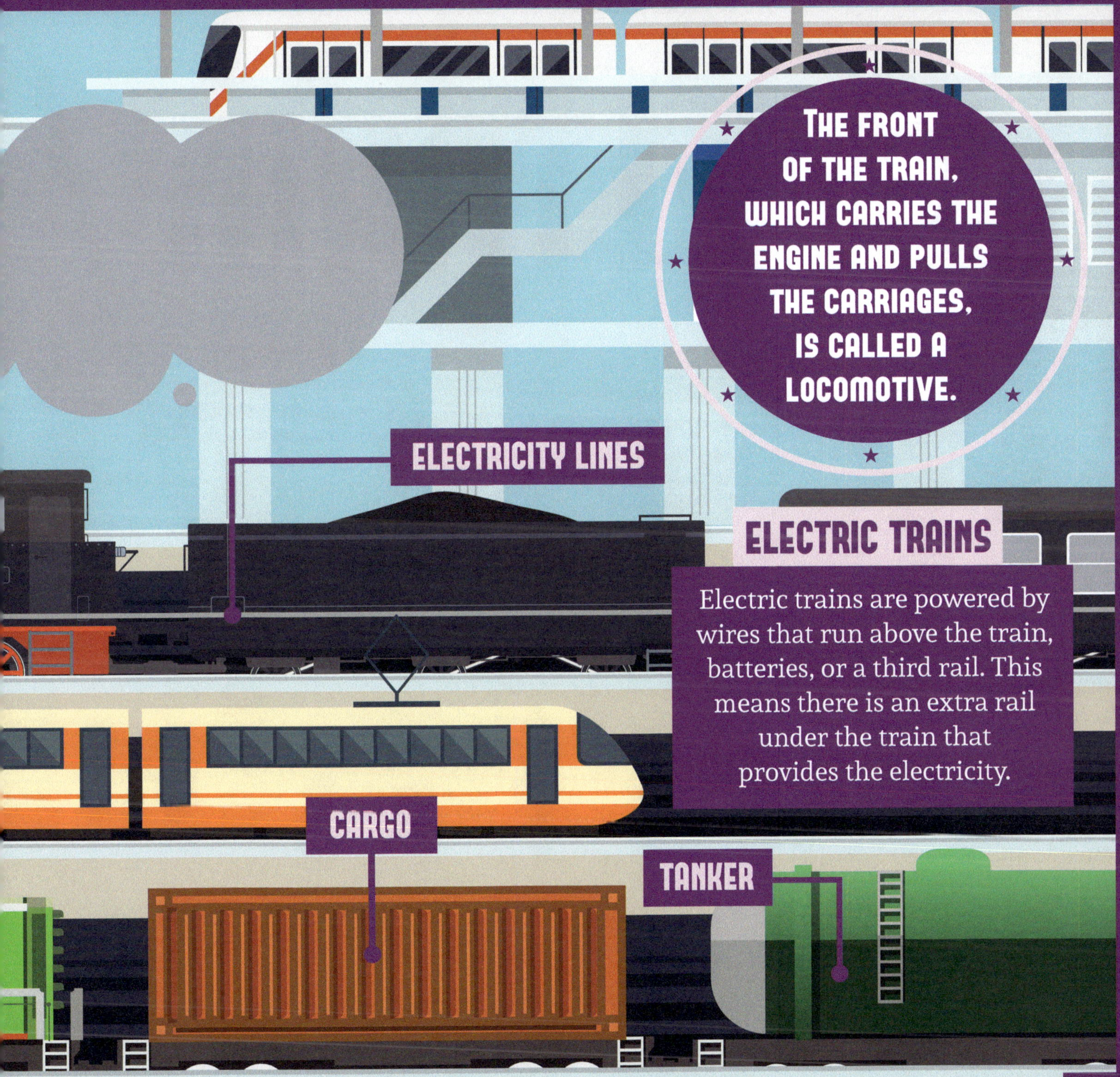

ELECTRIC TRAINS

Electric trains are powered by wires that run above the train, batteries, or a third rail. This means there is an extra rail under the train that provides the electricity.

LESSON 3: INSIDE A TRAIN

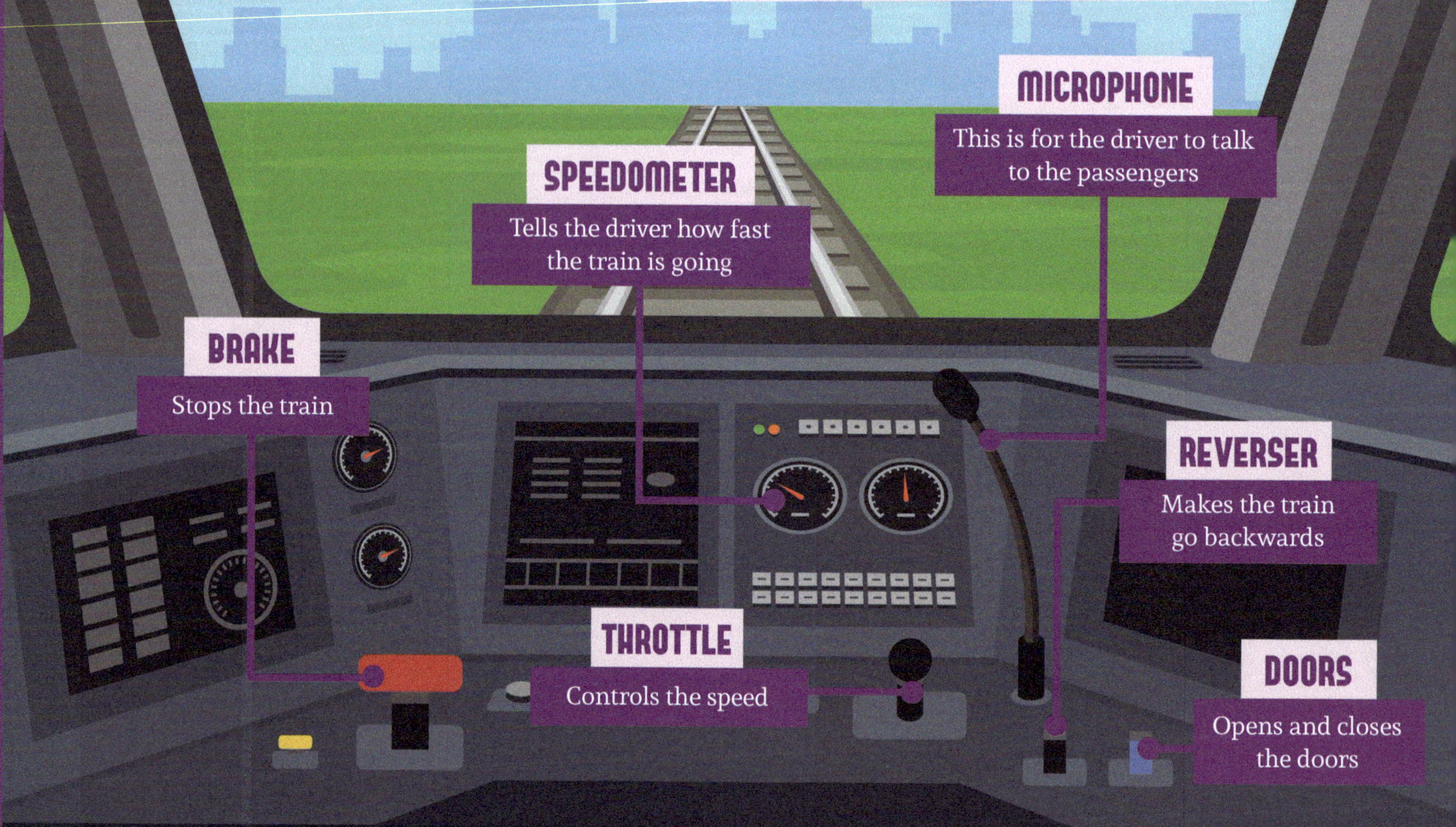

Inside a modern train, the controls are in the driver's cab in the front. The driver sits here, and all the controls they need are on the dashboard.

THE DEAD MAN'S SWITCH

The dead man's switch is a special switch that makes sure the driver of a train isn't away from their seat for too long.

60 SECONDS

If no controls are used for 60 seconds, an alarm goes off. The driver has to press a special switch to show they are still in control of the train. If they don't, the train will stop to make sure everyone is safe.

LESSON 4:

STEAM!

The first steam train was built in 1804 by Richard Trevithick. It had a speed of around 5 miles (8 km) per hour. By 1850, steam trains could travel at around 50 miles (80 km) per hour.

In 1938, the Mallard steam train set the world speed record for a steam train, traveling at 126 miles (203 km) per hour!

LESSON 5:

UNDERGROUND!

Many cities have trains that run underground, taking passengers across a city in minutes. **Systems** like this can carry millions of passengers each day, helping the streets aboveground to be less crowded and busy.

Underground train systems, such as the famous London Underground, use special maps like this one. They don't show real distances, and instead you follow the colored lines to know where you are going.

LESSON 6:

HYPERLOOP!

The trains of the future might not even need rails at all. One idea is the Hyperloop system. Pods (like train carriages) would ride on cushions of air through special tubes.

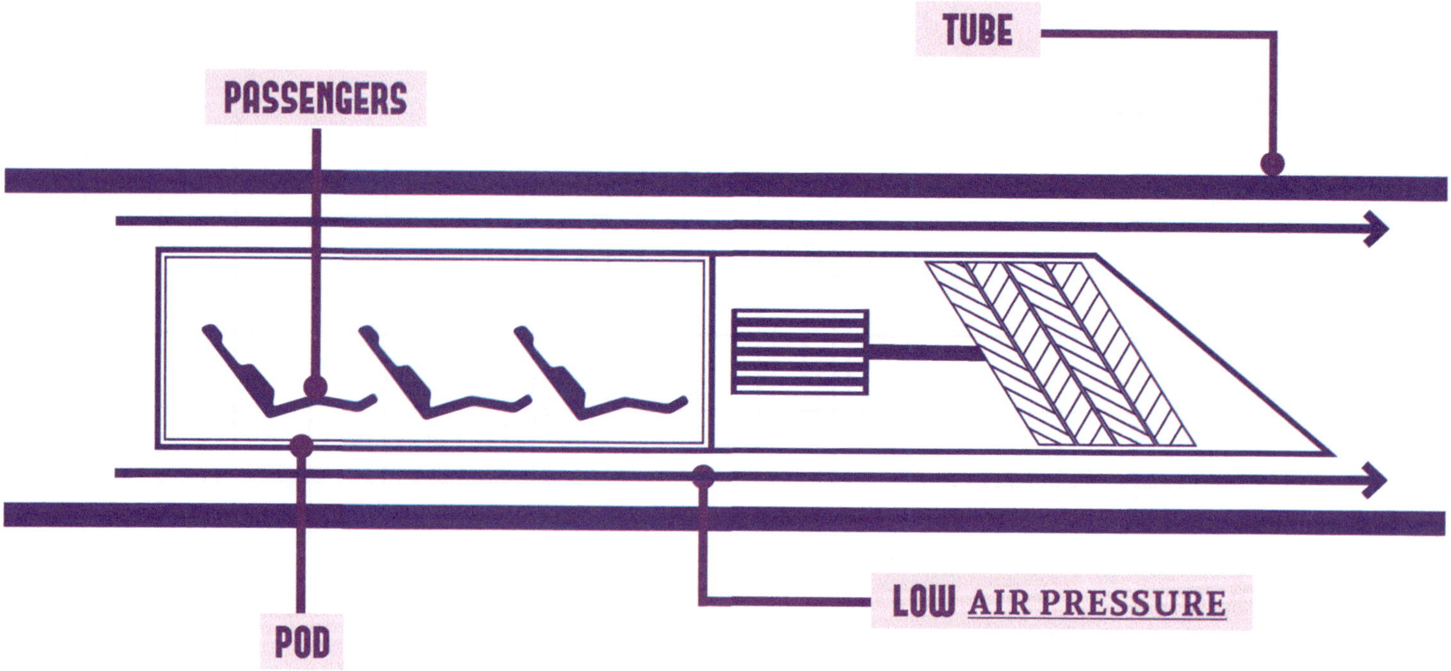

Inside the tube, the air pressure would be lowered. This means the train would be able to move through the tube very, very fast. Scientists think that Hyperloop trains could reach speeds of around 760 miles (1,223 km) per hour!

Lesson 7: Terrific Trains

What's an extreme way of making your train go faster? Stick a couple of rocket jet engines on it, of course! In 1966, Don Wetzel of New York did just that, and his train set a speed record of almost 184 miles (296 km) per hour. Now that's fast!

Did you know that the Hogwarts Express, as seen in the popular Harry Potter films, is a real train? The Jacobite Steam Train is in Scotland – and yes, you can ride it, but no, you don't have to find Platform 9 ¾ first!

DRIVING TEST

All aboard! It's time for your train-driving exam. Step up to the plate and pass with flying colors, and you'll get your Golden Horseshoe! (Check your answers on page 21!)

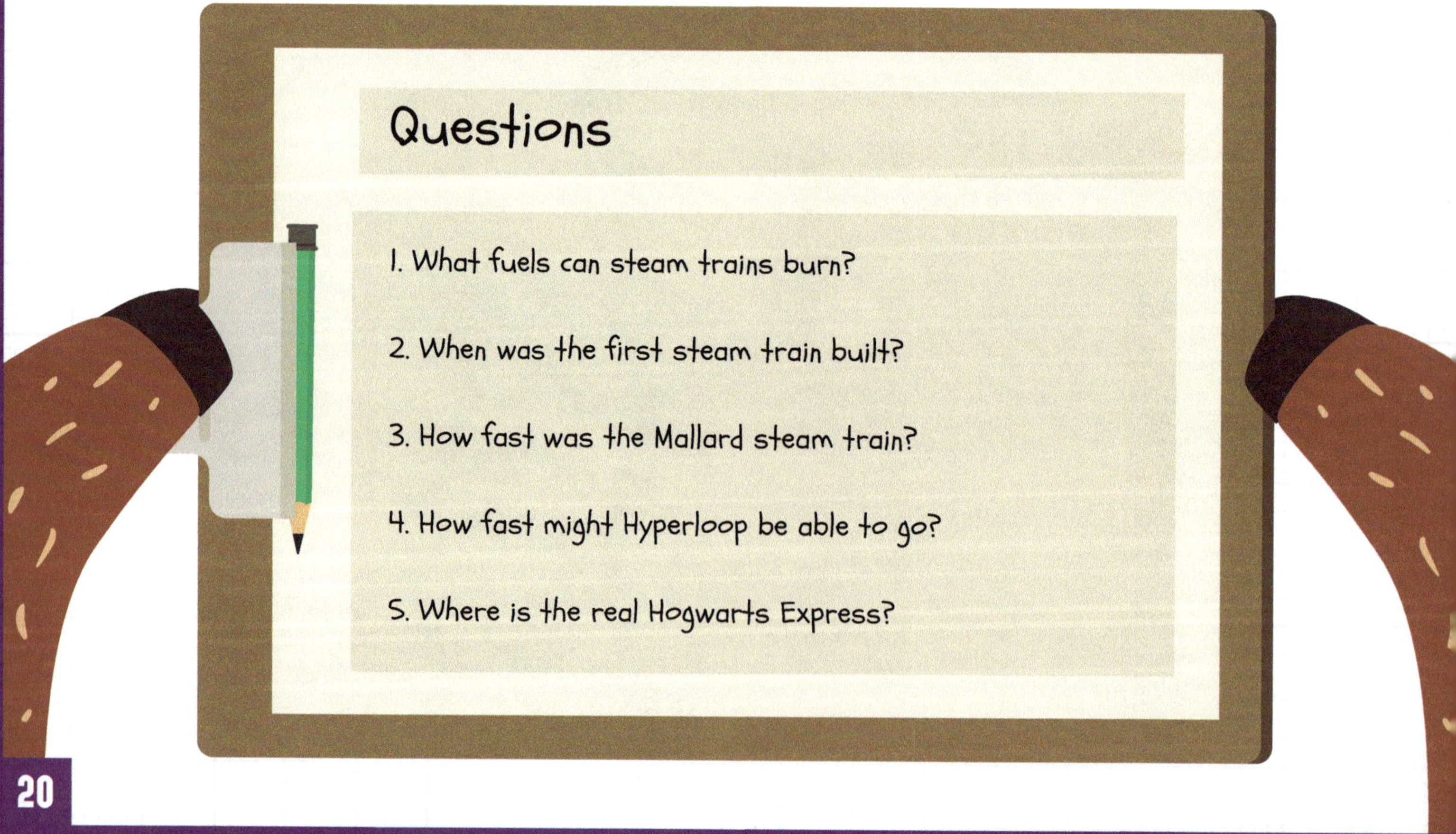

Did you get them all right?

Of course you did – here is your Golden Horseshoe. You are now a train-tastic driver, just like Peggy and me!

Answers: 1. Coal, oil, or wood 2. 1804 3. 126 miles per hour 4. 760 miles per hour 5. Scotland

Bonus Lesson:

CRAZY TRAIN

Trains aren't just serious business. There are also some that are here just for fun, so enjoy the ride!

STEP ONE

Line up

STEP TWO

Tickets, please

STEP THREE

Hold on tight...

STEP FOUR

...and SCREAM!!

GLOSSARY

AIR PRESSURE	the force of air pressing against a surface
ENGINE	a machine that uses electricity or fuel to make movement
FREIGHT	goods, things, or products carried in a vehicle or ship
FUEL	a material used to make heat or power
RAILS	steel bars that make tracks for a vehicle with wheels
SYSTEMS	sets of things that work together to do a specific job
VEHICLES	machines used for carrying or transporting things or people

INDEX